SHORT CIRCULAR WALKS
AROUND THE TOWNS AND
VILLAGES OF
THE PEAK DISTRICT

BY
JOHN N. MERRILL

MAPS AND PHOTOGRAPHS
BY JOHN N. MERRILL

a J.N.M. PUBLICATION

1990

a J.N.M. PUBLICATION,

J.N.M. PUBLICATIONS,
WINSTER,
MATLOCK,
DERBYSHIRE.
DE4 2DQ
© Winster (062988) 454
Fax: Winster (062988) 416

Concieved, edited, typeset, designed, paged, marketed and distributed by John N. Merrill.

© Text and routes - John N. Merrill 1990.

© Maps and photographs - John N. Merrill 1990.

First Published - June 1988
This edition - June 1990

ISBN 0 907496 76 8

Meticulous research has been undertaken to ensure that this publication is highly accurate at the time of going to press. The publishers, however, cannot be held responsible for alterations, errors or omissions, but they would welcome notification of such for future editions.

Typeset in - Bookman - bold, italic and plain 9pt and 18pt.

Printed by - Elgar Printing Ltd., Hereford.

Cover Sketch by John Creber - Hathersage church.
© J.N.M. PUBLICATIONS 1990.

An all British
product.

ABOUT
JOHN N. MERRILL

John combines the characteristics and strength of a mountain climber with the stamina and athletic capabilities of a marathon runner. In this respect he is unique and has to his credit a whole string of remarkable long walks. He is without question the world's leading marathon walker.

Over the last fifteen years he has walked more than 100,000 miles and successfully completed ten walks of a least 1,000 miles or more. His six major walks in Great Britain are -

Hebridean Journey....... 1,003 miles.
Northern Isles Journey......913 miles.
Irish Island Journey ....1,578 miles.
Parkland Journey........2,043 miles.
Land's End to John o' Groats.....1,608 miles.

and in 1978 he became the first person (permanent Guinness Book of Records entry) to walk the entire coastline of Britain - 6,824 miles in ten months.

In Europe he has walked across Austria - 712 miles - hiked the Tour of Mont Blanc, completed High Level Routes in the Dolomites and Italian Alps, and the GR20 route across Corsica in training! In 1982 he walked across Europe - 2,806 miles in 107 days - crossing seven countries, the Swiss and French Alps and the complete Pyrennean chain - the hardest and longest mountain walk in Europe, with more than 600,000 feet of ascent!

In America he used The Appalachian Trail - 2,200 miles - as a training walk, He has walked from Mexico to Canada via the Pacific Crest Trail in record time - 118 days for 2,700 miles. He has walked most of the Continental Divide Trail and much of New Mexico; his second home. In Canada he has walked the Rideau Trail - Kingston to Ottowa - 220 miles and The Bruce Trail - Tobermory to Niagara Falls - 460 miles.

In 1984 John set off from Virginia Beach on the Atlantic coast, and walked 4,226 miles without a rest day, across the width of America to Santa Cruz and San Francisco on the Pacific coast. His walk is unquestionably his greatest achievement, being, in modern history, the longest, hardest crossing of the U.S.A. in the shortest time - under six months (178 days). The direct distance is 2,800 miles.

Between major walks John is out training in his own area - The Peak District National Park. He has walked all of our National Trails many times - The Cleveland Way thirteen times and The Pennine Way four times in a year! He has been trekking in the Himalayas five times. He created more than a dozen challenge walks which have been used to raise more than £250,000 for charity. From his own walks he has raised over £100,000. He is author of more than one hundred walking guides; most of which he publishes himself, His book sales are in excess of 2 1/2 million, He has created many long distance walks including The Limey Way , The Peakland Way, Dark Peak Challenge walk, and Rivers' Way. He lectures extensively in Britain and America.

THE CRESCENT, BUXTON

CONTENTS

INTRODUCTION

The Peak District offers endless scope for walking. In the north are the moorland plateaux of Kinder and Bleaklow. Just south of them are the gritstone edges and ridges, while in the middle is the extensive limestone plateau. One of the joys of walking in this area is the rich and diverse history, surrounded by scenic splendour. While you walk you see historic halls, buildings, old mills and factories, and churches. These help to make the walk interesting and not just a fitness exercise.

My aim has simply been to work out a walk around a specific town or village. Not a long one—2 to 3 miles—so that you will come to the majority of historical features as you walk round. None of the walks are intended to be hurried—simply stroll round and take time admiring or understanding a feature. Stop at the church and discover for yourself its architectural aspects; inspect the gravestones, admire the font which could well be 1,000 years old; and look at the stained glass windows. The walks are a voyage of discovery and it is quite amazing the variety of items clustered in one small area.

In many cases I can only scratch the surface on the historical notes—places like Buxton need a book on their own. But I hope, brief though they are, they give a little insight into what you are looking at. There are numerous pubs on each walk, obviously, and these walks can be used for a leisurely afternoon stroll after closing hours. Alternatively they make excellent fitness circuits.

Whichever way you approach these short historical walks, I hope they provide you with a greater insight into the area. I hope too that they give you added stimulus to explore further and further on foot.

Happy walking!

John N. Merrill

JOHN N. MERRILL. WINSTER 1990.

ABOUT THE WALKS

Whilst every care is taken detailing and describing the walks in this book, it should be borne in mind that the countryside changes by the seasons and the work of man. I have described the walks to the best of my ability, detailing what I have found on the walk in the way of stiles and signs. Obviously with the passage of time stiles become broken or replaced by a ladder stile or even a small gate. Signs too have a habit of being broken or pushed over. All the routes follow rights of way and only on rare occasions will you have to overcome obstacles in its path, such as a barbed wire fence or electric fence.

The seasons bring occasional problems whilst out walking which should also be borne in mind. In the height of summer paths become overgrown and you will have to fight your way through in a few places. In low lying areas the fields are often full of crops, and although the pathline goes straight across it may be more practical to walk round the field edge to get to the next stile or gate. In summer the ground is generally dry but in autumn and winter, especially because of our climate, the surface can be decidedly wet and slippery; sometimes even gluttonous mud!

These comments are part of countryside walking which help to make your walk more interesting or briefly frustrating. Standing in a farm-yard up to your ankles in mud might not be funny at the time but upon reflection was one of the highlights of the walk!

The mileage for each walk is based on three calculations -

1. pedometer reading.
2. the route map measured on the map.
3. the time I took for the walk.

I believe the figure stated for each walk to be very accurate but we all walk differently and not always in a straight line! The time allowed for each walk is on the generous side and does not include pub stops etc. The figure is based on the fact that on average a person walks 2 1/2 miles an hours but less in hilly terrain.

CASTLETON - 4 Miles

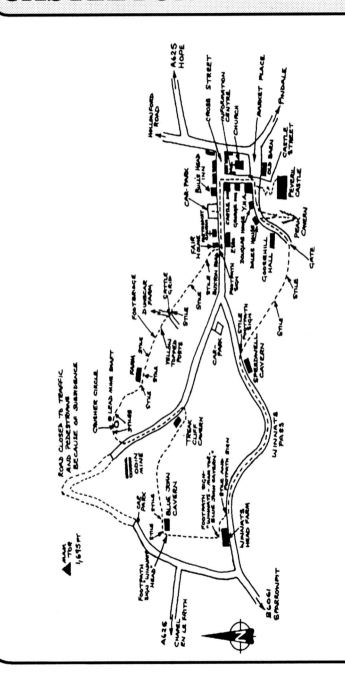

CASTLETON VILLAGE WALK
- 4 Miles - ALLOW 2 HOURS,
LONGER IF VISITING THE CAVERNS.

 O.S. 1:25,000 Outdoor Leisure Series—The Dark Peak.

 -- Just off the main street on the western side of the village.

Early Closing Day: Wednesday.

ABOUT THE WALK - Castleton is justly famous for its caverns and castle. This walk takes you to the four caverns and descends the impressive Winnats Pass, the scene of a gruesome murder in 1788. As you return to central Castleton you can extend the outing by ascending to the ramparts of Peveril Castle or exploring the attractive parish church. The village has several inns—some with legends.

WALKING INSTRUCTIONS - Return to the main road from the car-park and turn right. 200 yards later after passing the Esso station on your left, the Methodist Church on your right, turn right, as footpath signposted beside the house named "Fair Holme". Follow the well-defined and stiled path towards Mam Tor. After 1/4 mile cross the Dunscar Farm road via the cattle grid and continue ahead, guided by the yellow-topped posts. Walk in front of a farm before bearing right up the slope to the next stile. Continue on a good path to a small plantation and crushing circle before gaining the road. Turn left and descend slowly to the entrance steps to Treak Cliff Cavern. Ascend these to the cavern and follow the public footpath beyond as you ascend the slope. The path is defined and brings you to Blue John Cavern.

On the other side ascend a stile and bear left following the path to Winnats Head Farm. Turn left at the footpath sign in front of the building to the stile. Descend the road through Winnats Pass to Speedwell Cavern. Just beyond, as footpath signed, follow the path back to Castleton. Little over 1/2 mile later reach a track via a gate beside Goosehill Hall. Descend to Goosehill Bridge; just before, you can turn right and follow the path between the houses to visit Peak Cavern. Cross the bridge and ascend to the Market Place and Youth Hostel, passing Douglas House on your left. At the Market Place you can decide whether to ascend to Peveril Castle or turn left down Castle Street to the church and inns. Turn left at the bottom and descend Cross Street back to the car park.

HISTORICAL NOTES IN WALKING ORDER

CRUSHING CIRCLE—Dates from the mid-19th Century, and although used by Odin Mine just across the road it was used by others who brought ore to be crushed from several miles away. The crusher is 18 feet in diameter, 15 inches wide, 2 inches thick, and made from eight segments. The gritstone wheel is shod by a 2 inch thick iron tyre originally held in place by wooden wedges.

ODIN MINE—Said to have been used since Roman times, but nothing recorded until 1663 . Lead ore was extracted in the 1 8th Century at the rate of as much as 800 tons a year.

TREAK CLIFF CAVERN—Show cave opened to the public in 1935. Inside are some of the finest sights of stalactites and stalagmites to be seen in Britain. Equally impressive is the display of Blue John Stone, the only place in the world where it is found.

BLUE JOHN CAVERN—Numerous examples of Blue John Stone in its natural state. Originally, large pieces were mined for making vases, as can be seen at Chatsworth House. Today only small quantities are mined for making jewellry. The stone is a rare variety of fluorspar (calcium fluoride) and generally is found in veins of about 3 inches thick. The distinctive colouring is believed to be caused by iron, manganese dioxide, asphalt or bitumen.

WINNATS MURDER—It is said that in 1758 a couple known as Alan and Clara were on their way from Castleton to Peak Forest to be married. During their stay in Castleton a miner noticed the large amount of money Alan had. He told some others, and five miners hid in the Pass and awaited them. There they coldbloodedly murdered them and stole the money. The two bodies were thrown down an old shaft. The five were never convicted but all met strange deaths, and the last to die told the gruesome story on his deathbed many years later.

SPEEDWELL CAVERN—The shop contains a few relics of lead mining, and the saddle believed to have been on Clara's horse. The cavern is a former lead mine which ceased operating in 1790. To explore the spacious caverns you first have to go by boat for half a mile along a subterranean tunnel.

PEAK CAVERN—The largest cavern entrance in Britain, being 120 feet wide and 60 feet high. The remains of a rope-making concern lie on the entrance floor. Numerous large caverns can be explored.

PEVERIL CASTLE—Known as the Castle of the Peak, the remains date from Norman times. The prominent keep was built in 1157 at a cost of £135. The castle never saw a battle and in the 16th Century was rarely used except as a jail.

PARISH CHURCH—Dedicated to St. Edmund. Dates from the Norman period and has five Norman archways. The box pews date from the 17th and 18th Century and have the occupier's name carved on. The church is unusual in having an extensive library, which was used by the villagers. Included are two rare bibles— Cranmer's Bible dated 1539 and a Breeches Bible dated 1611.

CASTLE HOTEL—According to legend it has been haunted by a lady ghost. In 1603 a woman's body was buried under the stone doorstep.

GARLAND CEREMONY—On May 29th annually is held this ceremony in memory of the restoration of Charles II in 1660. The garland king rides on horseback encased in a 60 lb. conical flower garland. This is later hoisted to the top of the church tower.

CHRISTMAS LIGHTS—A more recent custom has seen the main street of Castleton festooned with Christmas trees and lights—from mid-November to January 6th.

✪✪✪✪✪✪✪

CRUSHING CIRCLE - ODIN MINE

HATHERSAGE - 3 Miles

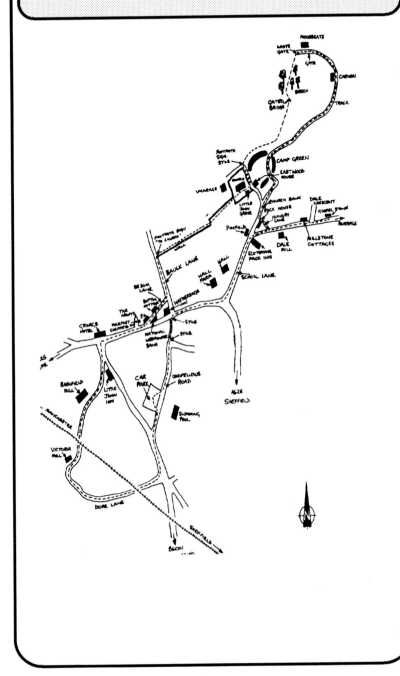

HATHERSAGE VILLAGE WALK - 3 Miles - ALLOW 2 HOURS

 O.S. 1:25,000 Pathfinder Series
—Sheffield—Sheet No. SK 28/38.

 Oddfellows Road—just off the B6001 Grindleford Road

Early Closing Day: Wednesday.

ABOUT THE WALK - Hathersage is extremely rich in local and national history. Many old buildings and industries remain, and on this walk you reach numerous places of interest and ascend above the village to admire its setting. On the walk you will pass old needle and button factories, see Little John's Grave, explore a magnificent 14th Century church, see exquisite brasses to the Eyre family, a Hall linked to Charlotte Bronte's novel—Jane Eyre—and see the village pinfold and pass numerous pubs!

WALKING INSTRUCTIONS - Turn right out of the car-park down Oddfellows Road to the Grindleford (B6001) road. Turn left, and 50 yards later right down Dore Lane. Follow this lane round passing under two railway arches and past the Victoria Mill and Barnfield Mill, before regaining the Grindleford road with the Little John Inn on your right. Turn left and right almost immediately onto the main street, the A625 road. 150 yards later walk up Besom Lane with the Post office on your left and the National Westminster Bank on your right. At the top turn left along Baulk Lane. 100 yards later turn right, as footpath signposted, and ascend the path to the church.

Pass through the Lynch Gate and turn left. 30 yards later turn right at the footpath sign and stile. Follow the curvature of the fence on your right to near a metal stile. Here bear left on a well-defined path which descends to a gated bridge. Cross and follow the path as it ascends through the beech trees to Moorseats Hall. Turn right at the white gate and pass through another gate shortly afterwards before gaining the track. Follow the track round to your right, past Carhead House, before descending gradually towards Camp Green and the metal stile you saw earlier. Follow the road as it zig-zags through Camp Green before reaching Church Bank. Descend another 20 yards before turning sharp left down a path into Hungry Lane .

Turn left and walk up the road to see Dale Mill, Millstone Cottages and the Gospel Stone. Retrace your steps and continue along School Lane to the A625 road. Turn right and 150 yards later, opposite the Hathersage Inn, turn left through a stone stile and regain, another 50 yards later, Oddfellows Road. Continue ahead back to the Car Park.

HISTORICAL NOTES - IN WALKING ORDER

VICTORIA MILL— Long single-storey buildings dating back to early last century. Originally used for the manufacture of cast steel wire and hackle pins. Later used for the manufacture of gramophone needles.

BARNFIELD MILL — From the mid-18th Century to late 19th Century Hathersage was a major producer of needles. At this mill Samuel Fox was an apprentice in 1815 and he later moved to Stocksbridge, near Sheffield, and started the now large steel works there. Another needle mill is Dale Mill, and a tunnel goes under the road to Eastwood Cottages and is believed to have been used for wire drawing.

MILEPOST—At the entrance to "The Crofts" an old milepost—Sheffield 10 miles—can be seen.

BUTTONS—An old three-storey building on Besom Lane, near the Post Office, was built, as the circular plaque details, by the Furniss family in 1781. The industry was short-lived, and in 1820 was described as "declining".

PARISH CHURCH—Dedicated to St. Michael's. The church largely dates from the late 14th Century, and is very closely associated with the Eyre family and Little John. The Eyre family were major landowners in the Hope Valley—more than 20,000 acres. In the 16th Century they built many fine Halls nearby—North Lees, Moorseats, Highlow and Offerton. Inside are several brasses to the Eyre family dating back to 1643.

LITTLE JOHN GRAVE—Robin Hood's faithful companion is reputed to be buried here. In 1784 the grave was excavated and a thigh bone 29 1/2 inches long was found—which would mean that Little John was eight foot tall. For many years Little John's cap and bow hung in the church. An inn in the village recalls his name, and two miles away, on Stanage Edge, Robin Hood's Cave recalls his companion .

MOORSEATS—Built by the Eyre family in the 16th Century. In 1845 Charlotte Bronte stayed in Hathersage at the vicarage; the vicar being Henry Nussey, the brother of her close friend Ellen Nussey. While she was here she visited the surrounding area and later wrote her famous novel Jane Eyre. Many of the places in the book have been identified with the area—Morton is Hathersage; Moorseats is Moor House where the Rivers' sister lived; and North Lees Hall is Thornfeld Hall.

CAMP GREEN—An earthwork sometimes known as Danes Camp, dating from the 9th Century.

GOSPEL STONE—The large stone is now part of a wall, but a plaque records its importance. Here on the Rogation Service, when walking the boundaries of the parish, the vicar would stand on the stone and offer prayers.

PINFOLD—One of the few left in Derbyshire. Here last century any straying animals were locked in until ownership was established. The owner then had to pay a fine to the parish before the animal was released.

SCOTSMAN'S PACK INN—An inn has occupied this site since the 14th Century; this one dates from 1912. As the inn sign portrays, the inn was on a major packhorse route—from Hathersage to Longshaw and on to Sheffield, and another via Stanage Pole to Sheffield. Inside is Little John's chair.

HATHERSAGE INN—Originally known as the Ordnance Arms, it was built by Major A.A. Shuttleworth in 1808.

LITTLE JOHN'S TOMBSTONE

EYAM - 2 Miles

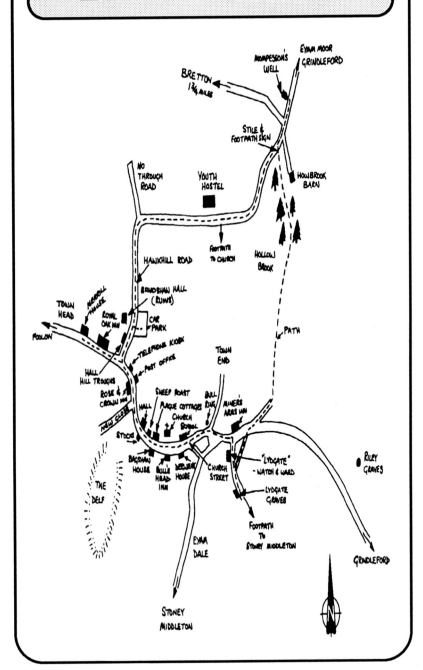

EYAM—2 Miles
- ALLOW 2 HOURS

 1:25,000 Outdoor Leisure Series—The White Peak— East Sheet.

West side of village on Hawkhill Road.

Early Closing Day: Wednesday.

ABOUT THE WALK - Eyam is a fascinating village full of history and immortalised by the Bubonic Plague that it suffered between September 1665 and October 1666. Many left the village at the start of the Plague, and out of the 350 who stayed, 267 died. The leader throughout these difficult times was the Rector, William Mompesson. He held the village together and isolated it from the surrounding places, enabling it to contain the disease. You first walk above the village to admire its setting and location, before reaching Mompesson's Well. Next you descend through woodland to the village and begin a historical walk, seeing many places of Eyam history associated with the Plague. Eyam, like several other limestone Peak District villages, has a well-dressing ceremony that takes place in late August. At the end of the well-dressing week a carnival and sheep roast is held.

WALKING INSTRUCTIONS - Turn right out of the car park and ascend Hawkhill Road. Follow the road as it curves round to your right, eventually passing the Youth Hostel on your left. Continue on the road as it swings to your left, passing a wood on your right and footpath sign—you follow this path later. Keep straight ahead at the road junction to visit Mompesson's Well. Turn round and retrace your steps to the stile and path sign, now on your left, and just past the drive to Howbrook Barn. Follow the path through the pine trees before descending to the village. In the final stages you descend a small lane, bearing left later to reach the road.

Turn right, and shortly afterwards left, along a lane into Lydgate. Turn left to visit the Lydgate graves a little way up on your right. Turn round and descend Lydgate to the road junction and entrance to the Miner's Arms Inn opposite. Turn left and walk along Church Street, passing the Bull Ring on your right, before ascending gently to the church on your right. Continue ahead past the Plague Cottages to the Hall on your right and stocks on your left. Further along the road you pass the Rose and Crown Inn before reaching the entrance of Hawkhill Road. You can keep ahead a short distance to the Royal oak Inn and Merrill House, before returning to the car park.

HISTORICAL NOTES—IN WALKING ORDER

HAWKHILL ROAD AND BRADSHAW HALL—The name of the road comes from the Bradshaw family who were keen falconers. The ruined hall was once the original manor of Eyam, and much of the stone has been used to build the nearby Eyam Hall.

MOMPESSON'S WELL—There were five places close to the village where money was left in vinegar water, to buy food, during the Plague. At this well Mompesson left letters detailing how things were in the village. Another stone with small holes drilled into it for holding money is approximately midway on the path between Eyam and Stoney Middleton.

LYDGATE GRAVES—Here can be seen the graves of the plague victims— George Darby on July 4th 1666 and his daughter, Mary, on September 4th 1666.

LYDGATE—This was originally the main road into the village, and a 'Watch and Ward' scheme was operated whereby the villagers kept watch on who was entering the village between the hours of 9 p.m. and 6 a.m.. In the house here Mary Rowland died on December 1st 1665 and Abel Rowland on January I5th 1666.

THE MINER'S ARMS—reminds us that Eyam was once a prosperous lead mining area. The inn was built before the plague in 1630. Inside can be seen details of a mock marriage that took place here in 1684. The rector of Eyam, Joseph Hunt, while somewhat the worse for drink, carried out a marriage ceremony with the publican's daughter, Anne. Unfortunately he was betrothed to a girl in Derby. The Bishop learned of the misdemeanour and instructed the Rector to marry Anne— which he did, but was involved in litigation for years.

BULL RING—The ring was originally in the middle of the road underneath a metal lid, but was removed to side in 1986. Bull baiting was once a popular pastime at wakes and carnivals. The bull's horns were protected and the bull secured to the ring, following which it was attacked by bull dogs. The custom was abolished by law in 1835.

BULL'S HEAD HOTEL—As the plaque outside the door details, the original name was Talbot Inn and in 1606 it had a thatched roof. In 1710 it was changed to the present name.

PARISH CHURCH—dedicated to St. Lawrence. Dates from the Norman period but was largely rebuilt in 1350. The interior and churchyard contain many items of interest, of which these are a few

INSIDE—Mompesson's Chair—made locally and belonged to Mompesson. Font—believed to be Saxon. Plague Cupboard—said to have been made from the wood in which the contaminated cloth arrived from London. Plague Register—records the dates and deaths of people during the plague.

OUTSIDE—Celtic Cross—8th Century, and one of the finest crosses in England. Catherine Mompesson's Tomb—tragically she died from the plague on August 15th 1666. Rev. Thomas Stanley's Tomb—Rector before Mompesson and his righthand man during the plague.

PLAGUE COTTAGE—Here George Vicars, a tailor, received the contaminated cloth. He became the first victim, dying on September 7th 1665. Opposite is Bagshawe House, where six members of the Sydall family died.

EYAM HALL—Built by the Wright family in 1676, and a descendant owns the building today.

STOCKS—Used for petty offences, such as drunkenness, up to 1815. They stand on the once cobbled market place. Down in the field behind the stocks is the Delf where Mompesson held open-air services during the plague to his dwindling flock. A commemoration service is held here on the last Sunday in August.

MERRILL HOUSE—No relation to me! Where Humphrey Merrill died on September 9th 1666. A solitary stone tomb in a field behind the house marks his resting place.

HALL HILL TROUGHS—Dates from 1588 and was originally part of a series of ten troughs and one of the first public water supplies in the country.

TIDESWELL - 2 Miles

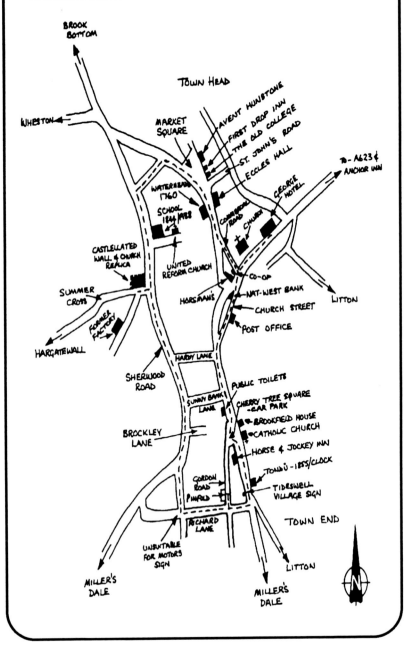

TIDESWELL—2 Miles
ALLOW 1 1/2 HOURS

 O.S. - 1:25,000 *Outdoor Leisure series—The White Peak - East and West Sheets.*

Cherry Tree Square.

Early closing day: Tuesday.

ABOUT THE WALK - Tideswell, affectionately called "Tidsa", was in the 17th Century one of the six most important towns in Derbyshire. There is lead mining in the vicinity, but its prominence stems from a transport and trading centre. Many of the old roadways and saltways pass through Tideswell, and in 1790 the Buxton-Sheffield stage coach came via Tideswell. Trading took place in the Market Hall and included needles from Hathersage, ropes from Castleton, shoes from Stoney Middleton and Eyam, and stockings from Litton. This accounts for the unusually large village today. This loop around the village takes you past a variety of buildings culminating in the Market Square with several historical buildings before reaching the finest church in Derbyshire, known locally as The Cathedral of the Peak. The village celebrates the well-dressing custom in June.

WALKING INSTRUCTIONS - Turn right out of the car park and walk along the main road, passing the Horse and Jockey Inn well to your right. A little later reach the village sign with Tondu House on your left. Turn right and ascend Richard Lane (almost immediately on your right is Gordon Road and a few yards along here is the village pinfold) to the crossroads, with an 'unsuitable for motors' sign ahead. Turn right and keep straight ahead back into the village along Sherwood Road. Follow this road for half a mile, passing Sunny Bank Lane and later Hardy Lane on your right. Shortly afterwards reach Summer Cross on your left. A short diversion here will enable you to see a former cotton factory and church replica on your right. Continue along Sherwood Road, and where you begin descending turn right down the side lane to enter the Market Square .

Continue past the Market Square with its First Drop Inn, Old College and Eccles Hall. Bear left down Commercial Road and turn left into the churchyard to visit the church. The tomb to the "Minstrel of the Peak" is against the wall to your left. Exit the church to the main road. A short walk brings you to the George Hotel. Retrace your steps and bear left down Church Street, regaining Cherry Tree Square .

HISTORICAL NOTES—IN WALKING ORDER

SUMMER CROSS FACTORY—Believed to have been called "Rising Sun", it was originally a cotton or velvet factory. The rooms had 30-feet long tables for cutting the material; business ceased in 1930, and it has since been used for a variety of uses including glove and knife handle manufacture.

HUNSTONE—Woodcarvers for more than three generations. Started in 1859 by Advent Hunstone. Some of his carvings—including the Vicar's Chair and Lectern —can be seen in the parish church. Their work is now in many ecclesiastical buildings in Britain, and some have been sent abroad to Canada and New Zealand. The building dates from the 17th Century, and was formerly the Marquess of Granby Inn.

ECCLES HALL—Built by Samuel Eccles, an Attorney, in 1724. In 1878 it became the home of the headmaster of the Grammar School and accommodation for boarders. It is now privately owned.

COMMERCIAL ROAD— Formerly called the Shambles. In the early 18th Century Tideswell was chosen as the best place to serve the Peak area for a house of correction. One was built here in 1711.

PARISH CHURCH—Dedicated to St. John the Baptist. The original church dates from the 12th Century, but rebuilding began about 1340 and was completed before the end of the century. Since then it has been little altered, and is the most complete 14th Century church in the country.

The interior is full of interesting features, including OCTAGONAL FONT—14th Century.

JOHN FOLJAMBE TOMB—near the altar. He died in 1358 and was a major benefactor to the church. The unusually large chancel was built because of a gift from him. The brass dates from 1875 as the original was stolen.

BISHOP ROBERT PURSGLOVE BRASS — is unusual for he is wearing pre-Reformation vestments. He died in 1579, spending the last twenty years of his life in Tideswell, during which time he founded the Grammar School.

SIR SAMPSON MEVERILL TOMB—in the centre of the chancel. He died in 1462 and was a notable soldier, being active in the Battle of Agincourt. In the Purbeck marble top are inscribed five crosses, which suggest it was once used as an altar.

LYTTON BRASS—They gave their name to the nearby village of Litton, and Sir Robert Litton, who died in 1483, was Under Treasurer of England in the reign of Henry VI.

BLACK OAK STALLS—Some of the original chancel stalls with 'misericords', now in the Lady Chapel.

OUTSIDE -
In the north-western corner of the churchyard can be seen the gravestones of William Newton and Samuel Slack.

WILLIAM NEWTON—was Manager of Cressbrook Mill and in his spare time wrote poems and hymns, earning himself the title of 'The Minstrel of the Peak'.

SAMUEL SLACK—was born in Tideswell in 1737, became a leading vocalist and even sang before George III. In later life he was an ardent supporter of the local Catch and Gee Club who met in the George Hotel. A sketch there shows him and others singing their hearts out.

THE GEORGE HOTEL — Former coaching inn dating from 1730, with venetian windows and oak panelled lounges.

TIDESWELL PARISH CHURCH.

BUXTON - 2 1/2 Miles

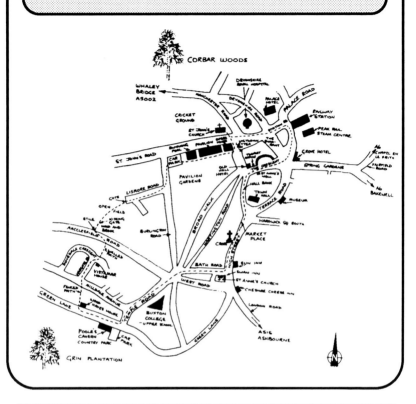

THE DEVONSHIRE ROYAL HOSPITAL, BUXTON

BUXTON—2 1/2 Miles
- ALLOW 2 HOURS

 1:25,000 Outdoor Leisure series—The White Peak - West Sheet.

 West side of Pavilion Gardens adjacent to St. John's Road and Burlington Road.

Early Closing Day: Wednesday. Market Day: Saturday.

ABOUT THE WALK - Buxton at over 1,000 feet above sea level is the highest town in England. The original town is above the Crescent—known as Higher Buxton, where the Market and Cross still remain. Down the hill is the Georgian Buxton, with Crescent, Devonshire Hospital, unique spa swimming baths and Opera House. On this walk you'll explore the extensive Pavilion and Gardens and pass many of the Georgian buildings before ascending to Higher Buxton and its remarkable St. Anne's Church. You cross to the southern fringe beneath Grin Plantation to see Poole's Cavern before weaving your way between houses and across fields to the car park.

WALKING INSTRUCTIONS - Walk to the end of the car park and join the tarmaced path through the Pavilion Gardens, passing the Swimming Pool and Pavilion on your right. Turn left at the end, and pass the Opera House and cross St. John's Street to St. John's Church. Turn right and cross Manchester Road and pass the Devonshire Royal Hospital on your left before walking up Station Road to the Railway Station. Turn right and descend the No Through Road down to the Quadrant. Opposite the Grove Hotel, cross over and walk along The Crescent, passing the Crescent building on your right, before the Information Office and Old Hall Hotel. Bear left and ascend Hall Bank to the Market Place. Bear right and continue along into High Street. In front of the Swan Inn, turn right into Bath Road. On your left is St. Anne's Church.

Continue along Bath Road to Macclesfield Road. Cross over to your right and ascend Temple Road—footpath-signed for Poole's Cavern. Follow the road round to your right to Green Lane. Opposite is Poole's Cavern. Turn right and walk along Green Lane for 120 yards to Wood Hayes House on your right. Just past it on the right is the fenced path down to Milldale Avenue. Cross this to your right and descend Hargate Road. At the bottom, cross Dove Dale Crescent to your right and descend another fenced then walled path to the Macclesfield Road. Turn left then right almost immediately through the stone stile and follow the path through woodland to a kissing gate. Keep on the path across the open field to a gate at the end of Lismore Road. Walk along this road to Burlington Road where turn left, and a short distance later on your right is the Pavilion Gardens and Car Park.

HISTORICAL NOTES—IN WALKING ORDER

SWIMMING POOL—Opened in 1972, the main pool holds 140,000 gallons of Buxton Spa water. Buxton was a very fashionable Spa for many years, and the water is known for its therapeutic qualities. The spa water has never failed, and a constant 200,000 gallons a day issue forth at a constant temperature—summer and winter—of 82 F.

PAVILION GARDENS—contain 23 acres of gardens and were opened in 1871. The buildings are good examples of Victorian design and workmanship. The Octagonal Hall was erected in 1875.

OPERA HOUSE— Built in 1903 at a cost of £25,000. Has recently been extensively restored and contains several painted ceilings. Theatres and shows are held here throughout the year.

VICTORIAN LETTERBOX—Opposite the Opera House and made in 1867. The hexagonal box is known as the Penfield after the designer J.W. Penfield. There are only 101 left in the country, and this is the only one in Derbyshire.

ST. JOHN THE BAPTIST CHURCH—Of classical style, and built in 1811 by Sir Jeffrey Wyatville. Inside is an exceptional organ by William Hill in 1897, and the stained glass windows are of particular note.

DEVONSHIRE ROYAL HOSPITAL—Formerly the Great Stables for the Crescent, it was designed by John Carver. The dome, one of the largest in the world, covers a surface area of 50 yards in diameter.

PALACE HOTEL—Built in 1868 by the 7th Duke of Devonshire and designed by Henry Currey; it is believed to have cost £100,000.

THE CRESCENT—Built by the 5th Duke of Devonshire between 1780-86, and rivals Bath for splendid architecture. The designer was

John Carr of York and the building, which has a curve of 200 feet and contains 380 windows, is reputed to have cost £120,000.

ST. ANNE'S WELL—Running spa water, which can be tried and does not have the usual unsavoury spa water taste, and is one of the reasons why Buxton Spa Water is so popular. The annual well-dressing ceremony takes place here in July.

OLD HALL HOTEL—One of the oldest buildings of Lower Buxton, and was known as Buxton Hall; it was owned by the 6th Earl of Shrewsbury, George Talbot. He and his wife, Bess of Hardwick, were the "jailers" of Mary Queen of Scots. She came here several times to take the waters; the last time was in 1584. The present building dates from 1670, and has a five-bay front with a Tuscan doorway.

MARKET CROSS—dates from the 15th Century, and the stocks would have been close by.

ST. ANNE'S CHURCH—Oldest church in Buxton, being built in the 16th Century. The date 1625 on the porch refers to the porch only. The interior has a remarkable tiebeamed roof, with painted ceiling above the altar and a magnificent array of stained glass windows. To the rear of the churchyard is the tomb to John Kane. He died quite tragically in Buxton and was a notable actor.

POOLE'S CAVERN—One of the Seven Wonders of the Peak (St. Anne's Well is another). Extensive show cave, floodlit throughout. Adjoining the site is 100 acres of woodland, now a country park. Footpaths lead to Solomon's Temple on Grin Low, half a mile away, providing extensive views over Buxton.

ST. ANNE'S WELL.

BAKEWELL - 2 Miles

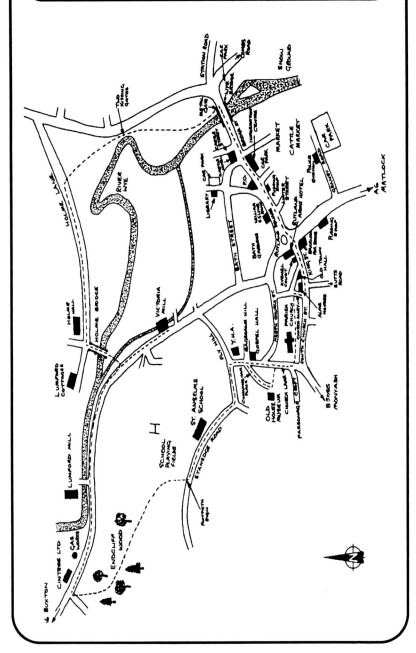

BAKEWELL—2 Miles
ALLOW 1 1/2 HOURS

 1:25,000 Outdoor Leisure series—The White Peak - East Sheet.

 1. Granby Road. 2. Behind Information Centre. 3. Off Bath Street. 4. Entrance to Combs Road.

Early Closing Day—Wednesday. Market Day—Monday.

ABOUT THE WALK - Bakewell is the administrative capital of the Peak District. A large weekly market is held on Mondays and in early August; one of the largest annual shows is held on the showground. The town has been immortalised by the renowned Bakewell puddings that originated here. On this short walk you will see where they were first made and pass a shop still making them to the original recipe. You cross one of the oldest bridges in the country, see a magnificent hall, two old mills, many old buildings, including the oldest—now a museum—and visit the parish church, extremely rich in Derbyshire legend — the Vernons of Haddon Hall. The well-dressing custom takes place in July.

WALKING INSTRUCTIONS - As there are several car parks in Bakewell, I have commenced these instructions from the main roundabout in Rutland Square, opposite the Rutland Arms. Walk along the road, past the Red Lion Inn and the Pudding Shop to the Information Centre and Bridge Street. Continue ahead to the bridge over the Wye, and on the left-hand side turn left through a metal gate and follow the path close to the river, to two kissing gates and onto Holme Lane. Turn left along the lane and pass the walled garden of Holme Hall on your right. Shortly afterwards, turn left and cross the packhorse bridge over the Wye and continue to the A6 road. You now turn right, but a short distance to your left is the Victoria Corn Mill.

Follow the A6 road past the entrance to Lumford Mill and on past the Gas Works and Cintride Limited. Just past this, turn left onto a rough track. Immediately leave it and ascend the distinct path through the trees of Endcliff Wood. Beyond the trees you cross the playing fields of St. Anselm's School to reach a path sign and Stanedge Road. Turn left and descend this road, past the school buildings to Fly Hill. Turn right and bear right shortly afterwards and follow Church Lane. A loop path here will take you, as sign-posted, to the Old House Museum.

At the entrance to Parsonage Croft, turn left into the churchyard. After visiting the Church, continue through the churchyard to your right. At Church Alley turn right then left past the Almshouses and Old Town Hall into King Street. Pass Avenel Court on your left and 30 yards later regain Rutland Square.

HISTORICAL NOTES—IN WALKING ORDER

RUTLAND ARMS HOTEL—Built on the site of the White Horse Inn, a renowned coaching inn. The present building dates from 1804. Seven years later in 1811 Jane Austen is reputed to have stayed here, and in her novel "Pride and Prejudice" a meeting between Elizabeth Bennett and Bingley is set here. In about 1859, the hotel cook misunderstood her instructions and created the now world-famous Bakewell Puddings. She put the jam in first and the egg mixture on top—it should have been the other way round, but the result is delicious.

INFORMATION CENTRE—Originally the Market House, built in the 17th Century .

WYE BRIDGE—Five-pointed arched bridge built in 1300, and one of the oldest bridges in the country.

HOLME HALL—Exceptionally attractive Jacobean building with mullioned windows and extensive walled gardens. Built in 1626 by Bernard Wells.

HOLME BRIDGE—Dates from 1664 and is part of an ancient bridle-way to Rowland and Great Longstone. Built into the parapet is believed to be a Roman altar .

VICTORIA MILL—Built in the early 19th Century as a corn mill. The 25-foot diameter mill wheel can be seen on the right of the building.

LUMFORD MILL —Formerly known as the Bakewell Mill, and built by Sir Richard Arkwright in 1778 for cotton spinning, employing 300 hands—mostly women and children. The mill burnt down in 1868 but was rebuilt. Now occupied by W. Fearnehough Ltd., who manufacture machine knives. Originally there were two water wheels here, the last one measuring 21 feet in diameter and 7 feet wide, in use until 1955.

OLD HOUSE MUSEUM—The oldest building in Bakewell—and a typical example of a wattle and daub Yeoman house. It now serves as a museum and has an extensive collection of Bakewell artifacts.

PARISH CHURCH—Dedicated to All Saints. Many remnants of the Norman building can be seen, but much of the building is early 14th Century. The octagonal tower and spire was built in 1340. The Vernon Chapel was built in 1360, and has a large tomb to Sir John Manners and Dorothy Vernon. Their love story and elopement from Haddon Hall in the 16th Century is one of the Peak District's most romantic tales. Nearby is a table tomb to Sir George Vernon, known as the King of the Peak, and father of Dorothy.

ALMS HOUSES—Built in 1709 for six single men. Prior to their building the occupiers lived in cells. The charity is a gift of the Manners family and dates from 1602.

OLD TOWN HALL — Built in 1602 and formerly the Town Hall and Courtroom. Later it became a library, a fire station, and in 1964 was a chip shop! It has now been restored to its former glory. Outside in the triangular square was held a butter market, and the town stocks would have been located here.

AVENEL COURT—Now an antique shop, but the building is mediaeval.

RIVER WYE BRIDGE, BAKEWELL
J.J.CREBER

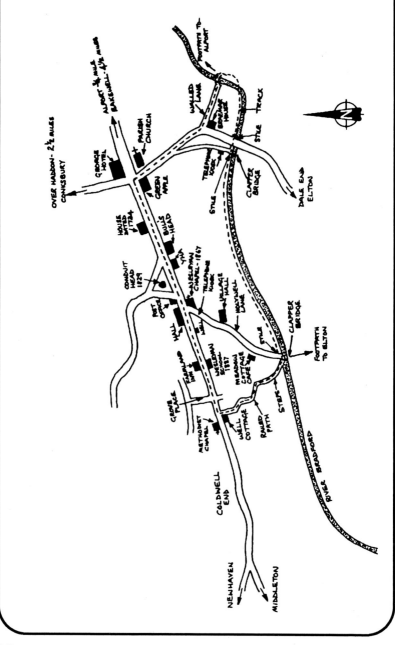

YOULGREAVE—1 1/2 Miles
- ALLOW ONE HOUR

 1:25,000 Outdoor Leisure series—The White Peak - East Sheet.

 No official one in Youlgreave.

Early Closing Day—Wednesday.

ABOUT THE WALK - Youlgreave was a former lead mining community, and in the 18th Century was among the richest areas in Derbyshire. This very short walk takes you to a variety of buildings—a 17th. Century Hall, and only a few yards away a magnificent Victorian building, now the Youth Hostel. Crowning the main street is the remarkable perpendicular-styled 15th Century church tower. The interior of the church is particularly notable, and contains a wealth of interesting features. You weave your way down through the western side of the village to the River Bradford. Here you enjoy a tranquil setting and see evidence of earlier transport routes—a packhorse bridge and two clapper bridges. Youlgreave, like many other Peak District limestone villages, celebrates the unique well-dressing ceremony at its five wells annually in late June.

WALKING INSTRUCTIONS - The walk commences from the entrance of Holywell Lane, opposite the Hall, but being circular you can start where you like. Facing the Hall, turn left along the Middleton road, passing the Farmland Inn on your right. Shortly afterwards pass the entrance to Grove Place and, just before the Methodist Chapel, turn left down the narrow road, with Well Cottage on your right. The road reaches a small square, where you bear left then right almost immediately and begin descending a railed path. Follow the twists and turns of the path, which becomes quite steep with steps as you near the River Bradford. Turn left and cross the end of Holywell Lane to a stile and follow the path on the lefthand side of the river.

A quarter of a mile later, pass through a stile and cross two roads to another stile and track beside the river. You soon cross over to the right before reaching a packhorse bridge on your left. Cross this and ascend the walled lane to the road beside Braemar House. Continue ascending to the church and main street. Turn left and walk along the main street past the Bull's Head and Youth Hostel back to Holywell Lane and Hall.

HISTORICAL NOTES—IN WALKING ORDER

OLD HALL—Built in 1650, it is a particularly fine limestone building with gables, mullioned windows and quarry-tiled roof.

WELL-DRESSING CEREMONY—Held each year on the nearest Saturday to June 24th—St. John the Baptist Day. There are five wells which remain dressed for a week, in colourful pictures of Biblical or topical scenes created by flower petals pressed into a clay base. The custom dates back to the water supply in 1829. The Wells are—Holywell Lane, Bank Top Well, Coldwell End, Fountain Well and Reading Room Well.

RIVER BRADFORD—As you walk beside the river, you pass two clapper bridges—early footbridges, and very few in Derbyshire—and cross a single-span packhorse bridge—evidence that packhorse teams passed this way. The river which is scarcely three miles long, is exceptionally clear and joins the River Lathkill at Alport. The Lathkill joins the River Wye, three miles away, near Haddon Hall. Upstream are several fishponds where kingfishers are sometimes seen. Along the bank sides clusters of yellow monkeyflowers can be seen growing.

PARISH CHURCH—Dedicated to All Saints. Part of the building dates back to Norman times, and of particular note is the font. It is very unusual as it incorporates a Holy Water stoup on the side. Originally this belonged to Elton Church, but when it was being rebuilt early last century it was discarded. In 1833 the Vicar had it brought over to Youlgreave, and it was used as an ornament in the vicarage garden. It was the next Vicar in 1838 who realised what a Norman treasure he had and placed it in its rightful place in the church. Elton soon appreciated their loss and had to make do with a replica. Near the south porch is an upturned font used as a sundial, dated 1752. The church tower was built in the 15th Century and is arguably the finest in the Peak District. The wooden ceilings in the nave and chancel are particularly fine.

In the sanctuary is the oldest monument, dating back to the 12th Century, to Sir John Rossington who holds a heart in his hand. Close by is an altar tomb to Thomas Cockayne, who died in 1488. The monument is noticeably small, as he died before his father. On the east wall of the north aisle is a monument slab to Robert Gilbert, dated 1492. In the centre is the Virgin Mary, with a man and his sons on the right. On the left is his wife and ten daughters. Not far away is a brass to Frideswide Gilbert who died in 1603 and was "a vertuous maide".

Like several other churches, including Baslow which has a dog whip on display, Youlgreave Church had in the 17th and 18th Centuries an official dog whipper. His duty was to whip the dogs out of the church in time for divine service. In 1604 he was paid 7p per annum for the task. In 1754 it was £1.00.

CONDUIT HEAD—Known as the Fountain and dated 1829, the tank has a holding capacity of 1,200 gallons. The village is one of the few to have its own independent water authority. Water is piped across the dale from a spring and serves about 400 homes.

YOUTH HOSTEL - Victorian building dating from 1887, which was until recently the local Co-operative shop. It has now been remodelled to a hostel.

YOULGREAVE CHURCH TOWER.

WINSTER - 2 Miles

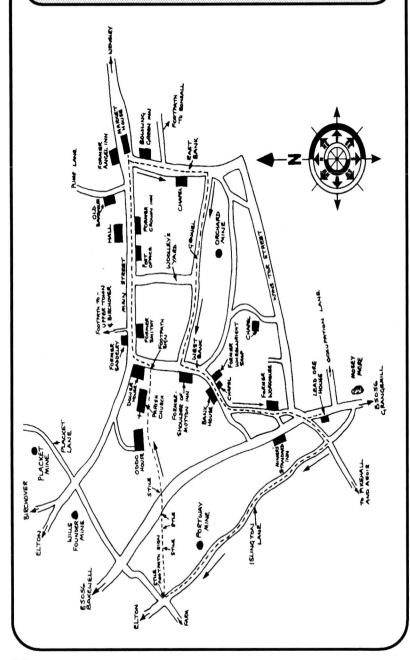

WINSTER—2 Miles
- ALLOW 1 1/2 HOURS

 O.S. 1:25,000 Outdoor Leisure series—The White Peak - East Sheet.

No official car park in Winster.

Early Closing Day—Thursday.

ABOUT THE WALK - Winster is an old lead mining village—once most prosperous—as illustrated by the large number of 18th Century buildings. The main street is all 18th Century and contains several fine buildings, including the Hall (built in 1628) and the 16th Century Market House. On the short walk you reach many of the key buildings and some of more than twenty inns that Winster had in the 18th Century. Winster still retains two unusual features. On Shrove Tuesday the annual pancake races are held in the Main Street. A Morris Dancing team maintains the tradition for Winster and has four dances bearing its name, including the Winster Gallup and The Blue Eyed Stranger. During the summer they often perform in Winster and the surrounding area.

WALKING INSTRUCTIONS - Since there is no car park in Winster, I have begun this walk from the Market House—Winster's most prominent landmark. Turn left and ascend East Bank. Pass the Bowling Green Inn on your left and later a Wesleyan Chapel, dated 1823. Almost immediately afterwards turn right along a "gennel"— a walled pathway. Follow this past the top of Woolley's Yard to West Bank. Turn left and ascend West Bank, passing Bank House on your right and, at the top of the steep hill, the former Workhouse on your left. To your right is the Miner's Standard Inn. Cross the B5056 road onto the Pikehall road. On your left is Lead Ore House and Mosey Mere. At the crossroads shortly afterwards, turn right onto the walled track known as Islington Lane.

Keep on this track for half a mile as you gradually descend to a farm track on your left. Turn right as footpath signposted through the stile and cross the stiled fields to the B5056 road. Cross the road to another stile and follow the path across the fields to the churchyard, passing Oddo House on your left. Walk through the churchyard, keeping to the righthand side. Walk along the lane for 20 yards to

West Bank. Turn left and right almost immediately and walk along Main Street, past the Hall back to the Market House.

HISTORICAL NOTES—IN WALKING ORDER

MARKET HOUSE—Originally the lower half, which dates from the 16th Century, would have had open arches for trading. The upper half is 18th Century and is believed to have replaced an earlier wooden construction. In 1906 it was in poor condition and given to the National Trust — their first property in Derbyshire. The upper storey was restored at a cost of £165. This storey is now used as a National Trust Information Centre, and is open on certain afternoons during the summer months.

BANK HOUSE—Dates from about 1580, and a plaque on the righthand side of the doorway records that it has been the home of the village doctor for more than 100 years.

FORMER WORKHOUSE—Built in 1744.

MINER'S STANDARD INN—was built in 1653, and over the doorway can be seen the dates and initials—E.P., E.P. and F.P.—stand for the names Edith, Ella and Frank Prince. In more recent times the initials have come to mean— Every person entering pays for a pint!

LEAD ORE HOUSE—The best preserved example in the Peak District. Here until the early part of this century local lead miners deposited their lead ore, down a chute, for safe keeping—like a bank's nightsafe. The building is constructed solidly like a bank vault.

MOSEY MERE—a rare example of water resting on a layer of volcanic rock in limestone country. It was used by the villagers of Islington and is surrounded by common land.

ISLINGTON LANE—The name is all that remains of a village that once existed here.

PORTWAY MINE—Known to have been in use in 1666, it was one of the richest lead mines in Derbyshire. Between 1746 and 1789, 31,850 loads of lead ore were produced, selling for £63,718. In 1789 a very rich vein was found, and in seven weeks a profit of £4,000 was made. Placket Mine was also very profitable, and in 1763 a profit of £7,750 was made. There are known to have been more than twenty mines in the Winster area in the 18th Century. In 1750 the population of Winster was over 2,000 with more than twenty inns.

Fifty years later, with the decline of lead mining, the population had reduced to 753—slightly more than today—and only two inns.

ODDO HOUSE—the third house to occupy this site.

PARISH CHURCH—Dedicated to St. John the Baptist. The tower was built in 1721, and the remainder was enlarged to its present size in 1883. Inside is a very unusual and thin quatrefoil archway. The clock was fitted in 1846 and cost £80.

DOWER HOUSE—Considerably altered over the years, but dates from the 16th Century.

THE HALL—Now an inn and restaurant, but was built by Francis Moore in 1628. A white lady is said to haunt the grounds! According to legend, a daughter of the house fell in love with the coachman. The parents would not agree to the marriage, so one day they climbed to the top of the building and, swearing true love, they held hands and jumped to their deaths.

MORRIS DANCING—Winster's own team can be seen performing in the village and neighbourhood during the summer months.

PANCAKE RACES — Held annually on Shrove Tuesday, and unique to Derbyshire. The races take place on the Main Street, and the pancakes are made to a special robust recipe.

THE MARKET HOUSE.

CROMFORD - 3 Miles

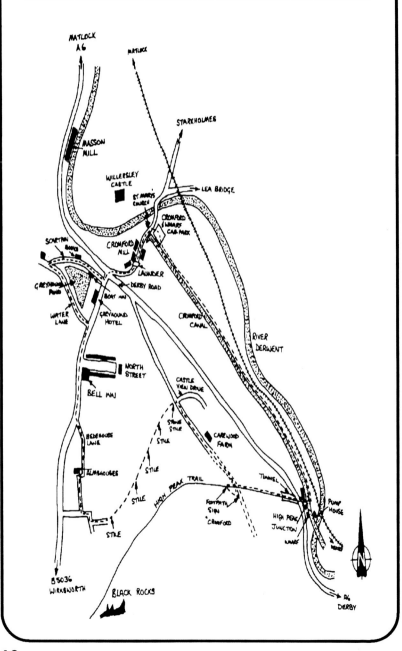

CROMFORD—3 Miles
- ALLOW 2 HOURS

 O.S. 1:25,000 Outdoor Leisure Series—The White Peak - East Sheet

 Cromford Wharf

Early Closing Day—Thursday

ABOUT THE WALK - In 1771 Richard Arkwright started a cotton spinning mill here which led to a huge industry in Derbyshire and the Midlands. He developed the factory system, and is today known as "The Father of the Factory System". On this walk you see at first hand many of his original buildings—mills and workers' houses—while walking beside a canal and ascending a unique railway line; now a pedestrian way. You pass several inns; can visit Arkwright's original mill; and go for a boat trip on the canal in the summer months.

WALKING INSTRUCTIONS - From the car park walk up to the canal and turn left and follow the tow path to the High Peak Junction, just over a mile away. Cross the bridge and begin ascending the High Peak Trail, passing through a tunnel under the A6 road. Before crossing the canal you can extend the walk a short distance to see the wharf and Pump House. Ascend the trail for a third of a mile, and shortly after passing a small building on your right you reach a path sign on your left—"Cromford". Leave the trail and follow the path past and walk through the tunnel under the trail and follow a walled path for the next 1/2 mile.

Pass Carrwood Farm on your right and enter a housing estate. Just before Castle View Drive on your right, leave the road and follow the distinct stiled path on your left for just over 1/4 mile. Keep straight ahead on the road and follow it to your right then left. Turn right down Bedehouse Lane, which becomes a tarmaced path in the middle. At the bottom turn right and descend the main road—"Cromford Hill" —to central Cromford. On the way you pass North Street on your right.

At the bottom of the hill turn left along Water Iane, and 300 yards later turn right along "Scarthin", on the right of Paul Mark Hairdressers. Turn left at the end to the A6 road. Cross over to the right and descend the road past the original Arkwright Mill to the start of the Cromford Canal and car park.

CROMFORD CANAL—Although opened after his death in 1793, Sir Richard Arkwright had been greatly involved. The canal was 14l/2 miles long and joined the Erewash Canal at Langley Mill and cost £80,000 to build. The canal enjoyed many years of use until the coming of the railway to Matlock in the 1860's. By 1900 it was closed to through traffic because of the collapse of the Butterley tunnel. The Cromford Canal Society and Derbyshire County Council have helped to restore this section of the canal. The Society operate boats on the canal and have restored the Leawood Pump House.

LEAWOOD PUMP HOUSE—To maintain the water level in the canal, this pump house was built in 1840 to pump water from the River Derwent. Inside is the original Graham and Co. beam engine. When operating it can lift between 5 and 6 tons of water a minute. Nearby is the aqueduct over the River Derwent.

HIGH PEAK JUNCTION—To link the Cromford Canal with the Peak Forest Canal at Whaley Bridge, a canal was proposed. But, because of the hilly terrain of the Peak District, it was not practical. Instead a railway with nine inclines was built and operating in 1831. The 33-mile journey took two days, and up each incline the wagons had to be hauled. It was never a viable railway and the last section closed in 1967. Since then a 17-mile section from here to Dowlow near Buxton has been converted to a pedestrian way. The incline you ascend is known as the Cromford Incline and is 580 yards long and a 1 in 9 gradient.

NORTH STREET—Cromford is now a Conservation area and much of the housing dates from the late 1 8th Century; being built by Sir Richard Arkwright for his workers. These three-storeyed buildings are among the finest examples of Industrial Archaeology to be found in England. Originally the upper floor was one long room, enabling the family to make stockings.

MILL POND—To feed water to Arkwright's original mill a series of five mill ponds were constructed—this is the last one. From here the water passes through tunnels and a channel before crossing the road in a cast-iron lauder (dated 1821) into the mill.

GREYHOUND HOTEL — Built by Sir Richard Arkwright in 1788. The splendid Georgian front has remained unaltered since then. Close by is the Boat Inn built in 1772.

MASSON MILL—Just along the A6 road and built by Arkwright in 1783. It is still operating today with more than 200 years of continuous use. The weir is unusual, being convex instead of the normal concave.

WILLERSLEY CASTLE—Sir Richard Arkwright lived in Rock House on the right of the mill but in 1788 began building his castle. Before work could commence a large boulder was removed at a cost of £3,000. By 1791 the building was almost complete when a fire badly damaged it. Arkwright died the following year and never took up residence.

CROMFORD MILL—Arkwright's original mill built in 1771. The mill operated almost continuously, with whole families working a twelve-hour shift. He was renowned for his modern thought and often paid workers when ill. In March 1786 he had 480 people working at the mill, with a total wage bill of £95.00 per week.

MILL POND IN CROMFORD.

LAUNDER INTO CROMFORD MILL.

WIRKSWORTH - 3 Miles

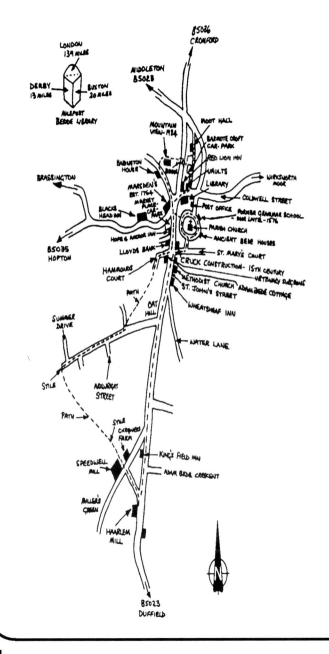

B5036
CROMFORD

MIDDLETON
B5023

LONDON
139 MILES

DERBY
13 MILES

BUXTON
20 MILES

MILEPOST
BEDE LIBRARY

MOOT HALL

MOUNTAIN
VIEW - 1924

BARMOTE CROFT
CAR PARK

RED LION INN

BABINGTON
HOUSE

VAULTS

BRASSINGTON

WIRKSWORTH
MOOR

MARSDEN'S
EST. 1764

LIBRARY

COLDWELL STREET

MARKET
PLACE
CAR PARK

POST OFFICE

FORMER GRAMMAR SCHOOL
DOOR LINTEL - 1576

BLACKS
HEAD INN

PARISH CHURCH

HOPE & ANCHOR INN

ANCIENT BEDE HOUSES

B5035
HOPTON

LLOYDS BANK

ST. MARY'S COURT

CRUCK CONSTRUCTION - 15TH CENTURY

HAMMONDS
COURT

VETERINARY SURGEONS

PATH

METHODIST CHURCH   ADAM BEDE COTTAGE

ST. JOHN'S STREET

OAT
HILL

WHEATSHEAF INN

SUMMER
DRIVE

WATER LANE

STILE

ARKWRIGHT
STREET

PATH

STILE
CHEQUERS
FARM

KING'S FIELD INN

SPEEDWELL
MILL

ADAM BEDE CRESCENT

MILLER'S
GREEN

HAARLEM
MILL

N

B5023
DUFFIELD

44

WIRKSWORTH—3 Miles
- ALLOW 2 1/4 HOURS

 O.S. 1:25,000 Outdoor Leisure Series—The White Peak - East Sheet.

Market Place and Barmote Croft.

Market Day—Tuesday.

ABOUT THE WALK— Wirksworth was once the centre of a vast lead-mining area, whose prosperity is reflected in the present buildings. Recently, much of the architectural heritage of the town has been restored. Cotton and tape works are on the fringe of the town. On the walk you see many of the main buildings and a remarkable Moot Hall, where the lead mining disputes were settled. You cross fields to see two mills and an area associated with Adam Bede, George Eliot's renowned novel. As you wander back past a mixture of modern and old buildings you reach the church, which houses an unusually interesting array of historical items. Wirksworth celebrates the well dressing custom in June and the unusual custom of "Church clipping" in early September.

WALKING INSTRUCTIONS - Starting from the Market Place, cross the road to the Library and Red Lion Inn. Turn right down Coldwell Street and left almost immediately beside The Vaults and into the car park in front of Barmote Croft. Exit onto the lane at the top righthand corner of the car park and walk straight ahead to the Moot Hall, passing a walled path on your left just before it. After seeing the Hall turn round and turn right almost immediately into the path. Follow this as it turns sharp left to a bridge over the main road. Ascend beyond Mountain View house on your left to a narrow road. Turn left and descend this, past Babington House to the Market Place. Keep on the main road and descend into St. John's Street, passing the Hope and Anchor Inn and later Lloyds Bank on your right. In front of the Vetenery practise, turn right along Hammonds Court. Keep left later and cross a field on a defined path to a road.

Turn right and walk along the road, passing Arkwright Street on your left and, almost at the road end, Summer Drive on your right. At the end of the road go through the stile on your left and walk to your left close to the edge of the field. Keep the housing estate on your left, and just beyond it reach a stile and track. Continue ahead and descend past Speedwell Mill on your right. Keep straight ahead and cross the minor road, and walk along the road to the main road. A little way to your right is Haarlem Mill . Turn left and walk along the main road hack to Wirksworth, passing the King's Field Inn on your left and later the Wheatsheaf Inn on your right. Opposite the Vetenary practise, with the 'cruck construction' just ahead, turn right into St. Mary's Court - to your right is the Adam Bede cottage .20 yards later turn left and enter the circular path around the church. Exit one of the openings on the left (west side) to return you to the Market Place.

HISTORICAL NOTES—IN WALKING ORDER.

MARKET PLACE—Wirksworth was, in the 18th Century, the third largest town in the county. With the decline of lead mining it became less important, and by 1901, with a population of 3,807, was 35th in the county. The market is held on Tuesdays and dates from 1397.

THE LIBRARY—The building, which forms parts of the Town Hall, is in Italianate style and dates from 1873 . Outside is an early nineteenth-century milepost.

RED LION INN—Former coaching inn, with central coach entrance. The front was built in 1750.

MOOT HALL—Built in 1814 for the settlement of mining disputes. An earlier Barmote court existed in the Market Place. The carved tablets on the front of the building depict the various tools used in lead mining.

BABINGTON HOUSE—Magnificent mullioned building, recently restored. Known as the Babington House for its association with the Babington family at Dethick, five miles away. Anthony Babington was executed in 1586 for his part in the famous Babington Plot to release Mary, Queen of Scots.

LLOYDS BANK—A local, John Toplis, started a bank here in 1780, and it was for a while the only bank between Derby and Chesterfield.

SPEEDWELL MILL — Former cotton spinning mill built by Sir Richard Arkwright in 1780. Nine years later it had 200 employees. In 1852 it was a tape mill .

HAARLEM MILL—The mill has had a variety of uses. In the 15th Century it was a waulk mill for fulling cloth. Later corn milling was begun, and in 1780 a cotton spinning mill—part of Sir Richard Arkwright's empire. In the 19th Century it was used for tape weaving. Red tape made Wirksworth famous.

KING'S FIELD INN—Although a new inn, the name recalls that Wirksworth was once the centre of a lead mining area—73,800 acres—known as the King's Field. In the 9th Century the area was owned by Repton Abbey, and rent was paid in the form of lead. When the Abbey was destroyed by the Danes in 875 AD, the area came under the ownership of the Danish King.

ADAM BEDE COTTAGE—Former home of Samuel and Elizabeth Evans, who in George Eliot's book—Adam Bede—were known as Adam Bede and Dinah Morris. Elizabeth Evans was a lay preacher who preached in the Methodist Church and was often named Dinah Bede. She was George Eliot's aunt and is buried in the parish churchyard. In the book Wirksworth is named Snowfield.

CRUCK CONSTRUCTION—shows beams resting on stones; believed to be 15th Century, and was discovered in 1971.

ALMSHOUSES—Founded in 1584 and built soon afterwards.

FORMER GRAMMAR SCHOOL—Founded in 1584 as a Free Grammar School by Anthony Gell. It is now a wood-carving factory. The present Gothic-styled building dates from 1828. The doorway lintel on the right bears the date 1576 and came from a much earlier building.

PARISH CHURCH—dedicated to St. Mary the Virgin.
The cruciform-shaped church dates from the 13th Century and is one of the largest in the county, being unique by having a circular path around the outside. The interior contains the Blackwall brass dated 1525 and four monuments to the Gell family, from nearby Hopton Hall. They were great benefactors of the town and Sir John Gell, who died in 1671, became notorious as the Parliamentary Governor of Derbyshire and was the first baronet of the family. The font is Norman and lead-lined. The pride of place goes to the Wirksworth Stone, believed to be a coffin lid dated about 800 AD . The stone was found by accident in 1820 when paving was removed in front of the altar.

TISSINGTON - 1 1/2 Miles

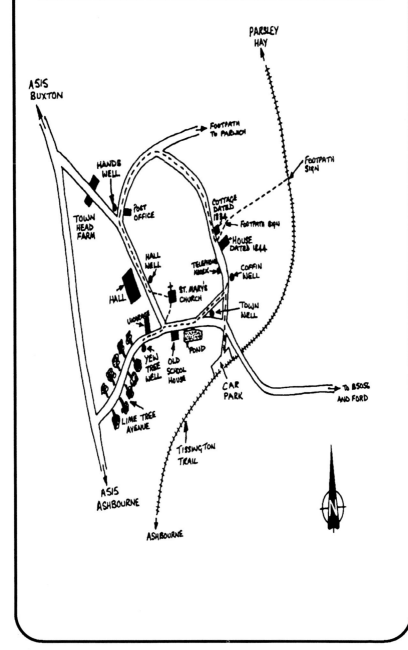

TISSINGTON—1 1/2 Miles
- ALLOW 1 1/2 HOURS

 O.S. 1:25,000 Outdoor Leisure Series—The White Peak - East Sheet.

 —Beside Tissington Trail.

ABOUT THE WALK - Tissington is beyond doubt one of the most attractive villages of the Peak District. The quiet peaceful location and the uncluttered scene create a place of timeless beauty. This short walk is not to be hurried and, like a good wine, it should be savoured slowly. The village is renowned for its well-dressing ceremony in May, and it is a colourful occasion. You sec all five wells and observe the magnificent Hall, built and still owned by the Fitzherbert family. Opposite is the parish church dating back to Norman times, and to return to the car park you pass the village pond before regaining the Tissington Trail. This is one village which does not have an inn; instead there is a village tea shop.

WALKING INSTRUCTIONS - From the car park follow the Tissington Trail to your left under the road bridge and keep on the trail for the next 1/4 mile. As footpath-signposted, turn left and follow the path across the fields to Tissington, three fields away. Reach the village road after passing the house on your left with the date 1844 and the cottage on your right dated 1834. Turn right and follow the road, which after 1/4 mile curves to your left. Beyond reach the Post Office on your left and Hands Well on your right.

Turn left and gently descend the main street, passing the I hall on your right and Hall Well on your left. Shortly afterwards turn left and ascend the path to the church. Return to the main street and turn right to see Yew Tree Well. Retrace your steps, pass the Old School House to the village pond on your right and Town Well on your left. Keep left and follow the road past the houses on your left to another road. Turn left to Coffin Well. Turn round and follow this road back to your earlier road. Cross over and descend the road to the car park.

TISSINGTON CHURCH—dedicated to St. Mary.
Dates from Norman times, with tower, font and typanum from this period. The interior contains some exceptionally fine stained glass windows and monuments to the Fitzherbert family. The communion rails date from the 16th Century. The pulpit incorporates a priest's

HISTORICAL NOTES—IN WALKING ORDER

TISSINGTON TRAIL—In 1971 a section of railway line was officially opened as a pedestrian way, and runs for 13 miles between Ashbourne and Parsley Hay. The line dates back to 1899 when a railway began operating between Ashbourne and Buxton; part of the London and North-Western Railway. Tissington had its own station—now the car park—and apart from carrying passengers the line carried considerable freight—limestone from the surrounding quarries, and milk. Passenger service ceased in 1954 but sections remained in use until 1967. Apart from walking the trail, you can hire bicycles from Ashbourne or Parsley Hay and cycle all or part of the trail and the adjoining High Peak Trail.

WELL DRESSING—There are five wells in Tissington—Hands Well, Hall Well, Yew Tree Well, Town Well and Coffin Well—you reach all of them. The origin of well dressing is still debatable, but is known to have started here in 1350 following the Black Death of 1348-49. While many of the surrounding villages suffered, Tissington did not because of the purity of its well. As a way of thanks the wells are dressed annually and Tissington is among the first, each year on Ascension Day. A wooden frame supporting a clay base is erected at the well. Onto the clay are pressed flower petals and leaves to create a topical or biblical scene. The result is a stunning picture, and after being blessed by the local vicar remains in place for a week. The custom takes place only in the Peak District limestone area, and throughout the summer months other villages such as Eyam, Bakewell, Buxton and Youlgreave have their ceremonies. In Tissington, Hall Well is sometimes known as Cup and Saucer Well, and both Hands Well and Yew Tree Well, which used to be known as Goodwin Well, are names of local farmers.

TISSINGTON HALL—The building dates from 1609 and was built by Francis Fitzherbert. The wrought iron gates close to the road were made by Robert Bakewell of Derby in 1720. The baronetcy dates from 1783 when Sir William Fitzherbert was made a baronet by George III for his services as Gentleman Usher. The two literary giants, Drs. Johnson and Boswell, stayed here in the 18th Century. The library wing was added in 1910. The stable clock dates from the mid-18th Century and was made in Ashbourne; it still keeps accurate time. The Hall gardens are open twice a year under the National Gardens Scheme.

TISSINGTON - WELL DRESSING.

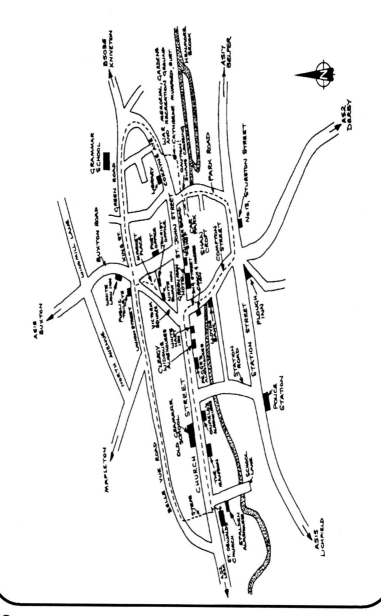

ASHBOURNE—2 Miles
- ALLOW 2 HOURS

 O.S. 1:25,000 Pathfinder Series Sheet No. SK 04/14—Ashbourne and the Churnet Valley.

Shaw Croft off Park Road—east side of town.

Early Closing Day: Wednesday.

Market Days: Thursday and Saturday.

ABOUT THE WALK - Ashbourne, the Gateway to Dove Dale, is one of the most historical towns of the area. Not only is it famed for its Shrovetime football match, but Church Street is the finest 18th Century street in Derbyshire. You start the walk at Shaw Croft, where the football is thrown up, before passing the birthplace of Catherine Mumford, who later became with her husband William Booth the founders of the Salvation Army. You continue on through the "village" of Compton before walking along Church Street, with its 18th Century houses, Almshouses and Old Grammar School, to the parish church. You curve back above the church to see the historic Market Place before gaining the gardens and a monument to Catherine Mumford, just before the car park.

WALKING INSTRUCTIONS - Turn right out of the car park and walk along Park Road. Turn right onto Sturston Road and right again into Compton Street. Follow this over the Henmore Brook into Dig Street. At the end turn left along Church Street—on your right is the Green Man Hotel and almost ahead is Victoria Square. Follow Church Street past the Almshouses, Old Grammar School and Mansion to the parish church. Turn right and ascend the steps to Belle View Road. Turn right and follow this road to Union Street, which you keep on to the end of the Market Place. Cross Buxton Road into King Street and onto Green Lane. Turn right down the curving Cokayne Avenue. Just before reaching the library on your right, leave the road by your left and enter the memorial gardens. Follow the path through the grounds to Park Road. Cross, and almost opposite is Shaw Croft car park.

HISTORICAL NOTES—IN WALKING ORDER

SHROVETIDE FOOTBALL—Really a free for all between "The Up'ards and Down'ards". The town of Ashbourne is split in half by the Henmore Brook, and depending on where you were born decides which team you are in. "The Up'ards" are born to the north of the river, and "The Down'ards" to the south. The goals are the site of Sturton Mill and Clifton Mill, three miles apart. It is rare for more than one goal to be scored!

NO. 13 STURSTON ROAD—Birthplace of Catherine Mumford, who later married William Booth. They established the Salvation Army in 1878. A bust to Catherine Booth is in the Memorial Gardens, which you walk through at the end of the walk.

COMPTON—The original town of Ashbourne was always to the north of the Henmore Brook. Compton on the south side was a separate village with its own market, as can be seen by the wide street. It was not until 1873 that Compton came under the jurisdiction of Ashbourne.

LLOYDS BANK—Dates from the late 18th Century, and was formerly the town house of the Beresford family of nearby Fenny Bentley.

GREEN MAN HOTEL—Former coaching inn with covered court, dating from the mid-18th Century. The inn sign is one of only six left in the county; known as a gallows sign, it commemorates the amalgamation of two inns—The Green Man and the Black's Head in 1825.

NO. 4 VICTORIA SQUARE—Now a butcher's shop, but was once an inn named The Tiger. The building dates from the 16th Century, and part of its timber frame can be seen facing Tiger Yard.

CLERGY WIDOWS ALMSHOUSES—Built in 1753 and founded under the Will of Nicholas Spalden—"four neat and pretty houses for entertaining the widows of four clergymen of the Church of England". Now private flats.

PEGGE'S ALMSHOUSES—Built from local sandstone in 1669.

OWFIELD'S ALMSHOUSES—Built in 1640, the upper storey being added in 1840.

OLD GRAMMAR SCHOOL—Built between 1585-1610 and now used as a boys' boarding house. The Queen Elizabeth's Grammar School was founded by Queen Elizabeth the First in 1585 and opened as a school in 1603.

THE MANSION—Now used as a girls' boarding school and dates from 1685, although altered by Robert Adam in the early 1760s.

PARISH CHURCH—dedicated to St. Oswald. Often referred to as the "Pride of the Peak", the church's spire with offset clock is a familiar landmark. The spire is 215 feet high and weighs 300 tons. The building dates from the 13th Century and was consecrated in 1241. The interior contains a wealth of monuments to local families, such as the Knivetons, Cokaynes, Bradbournes and the Boothbys. The latter have a marble figure to Penelope Boothby, who died aged six in 1791. She is said to have been able to speak four languages, and these are inscribed on her tomb.

SPALDEN'S ALMSHOUSES—Adjoining the churchyard and founded by Nicholas Spalden, who died in 1713. The Almshouses are for married couples and were built in 1723.

MARKET PLACE—The market dates from 1257 and is still held here on a Thursday and Saturday. The market type cross was built by Francis Wright (1806-1873). He lived at nearby Osmanton Manor, and was owner of the Butterley ironworks.

ASHBOURNE PARISH CHURCH.

EYAM - CELTIC CROSS.

**WIRKSWORTH - MOOT
HALL TABLET.**

**EYAM - MINERS' ARMS
INN NOTICE.**

EQUIPMENT NOTES

- Some personal thoughts

BOOTS - preferably with a full leather upper, of medium weight, with a vibram sole. I always add a foam cushioned insole to help cushion the base of my feet.

SOCKS - I generally wear two thick pairs as this helps minimise blisters. The inner pair are of loop stitch variety and approximately 80% wool. The outer are a thick rib pair of approximately 80% wool.

WATERPROOFS - for general walking I wear a T shirt or cotton shirt with a cotton wind jacket on top. You generate heat as you walk and I prefer to layer my clothes to avoid getting too hot. Depending on the season will dictate how many layers you wear. In soft rain I just use my wind jacket for I know it quickly dries out. In heavy or consistant rain I slip on a neoprene lined gagoule, and although hot and clammy it does keep me reasonably dry. Only in extreme conditions will I don overtrousers, much preferring to get wet and feel comfortable. I never wear gaiters!

FOOD - as I walk I carry bars of chocolate, for they provide instant energy and are light to carry. In winter a flask of hot coffee is welcome. I never carry water and find no hardship from not doing so, but this is a personal matter! From experience I find the more I drink the more I want and sweat. You should always carry some extra food such as Kendal Mint Cake, for emergencies.

RUCKSACKS - for day walking I use a climbing rucksack of about 40 litre capacity and although it leaves excess space it does mean that the sac is well padded, with an internal frame and padded shoulder straps. Inside apart from the basics for one day I carry gloves, balaclava, spare pullover and a pair of socks.

MAP & COMPASS - when I am walking I always have the relevant map - preferably 1:25,000 scale - open in my hand. This enables me to constantly check that I am walking the right way. In case of bad weather I carry a compass, which once mastered gives you complete confidence in thick cloud or mist.

REMEMBER AND OBSERVE THE COUNTRY CODE

 Enjoy the countryside and respect its life and work.

 Guard against all risk of fire.

 Fasten all gates.

 Keep your dogs under close control.

 Keep to public paths across farmland.

 Use gates and stiles to cross fences, hedges and walls.

  Leave livestock, crops and machinery alone.

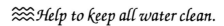 *Take your litter home - pack it in; pack it out.*

 Help to keep all water clean.

 Protect wildlife, plants and trees.

Take special care on country roads.

THE HIKER'S CODE

❀ Hike only along marked routes - do not leave the trail.

❀ Use stiles to climb fences; close gates.

❀ Camp only in designated campsites.

❀ Carry a light-weight stove.

❀ Leave the trail cleaner than you found it.

❀ Leave flowers and plants for others to enjoy.

❀ Keep dogs on a leash.

❀ Protect and do not disturb wildlife.

❀ Use the trail at your own risk.

❀ Leave only your thanks and footprints - take nothing but photographs.

OTHER BOOKS by JOHN N. MERRILL PUBLISHED by JNM PUBLICATIONS

CIRCULAR WALK GUIDES -
SHORT CIRCULAR WALKS IN THE PEAK DISTRICT
LONG CIRCULAR WALKS IN THE PEAK DISTRICT
CIRCULAR WALKS IN WESTERN PEAKLAND
SHORT CIRCULAR WALKS IN THE STAFFORDSHIRE MOORLANDS
SHORT CIRCULAR WALKS AROUND THE TOWNS & VILLAGES OF
THE PEAK DISTRICT
SHORT CIRCULAR WALKS AROUND MATLOCK
SHORT CIRCULAR WALKS IN THE DUKERIES
SHORT CIRCULAR WALKS IN SOUTH YORKSHIRE
SHORT CIRCULAR WALKS AROUND DERBY
SHORT CIRCULAR WALKS AROUND BUXTON
SHORT CIRCULAR WALKS IN THE HOPE VALLEY
40 SHORT CIRCULAR WALKS IN THE PEAK DISTRICT
CIRCULAR WALKS ON KINDER & BLEAKLOW
SHORT CIRCULAR WALKS IN SOUTH NOTTINGHAMSHIRE
SHIRT CIRCULAR WALKS IN CHESHIRE

CANAL WALKS -
VOL 1 - DERBYSHIRE & NOTTINGHAMSHIRE
VOL 2 - CHESHIRE & STAFFORDSHIRE
VOL 3 - STAFFORDSHIRE
VOL 4 - THE CHESHIRE RING
VOL 5 - LINCOLNSHIRE & NOTTINGHAMSHIRE
VOL 6 - SOUTH YORKSHIRE
VOL 7 - THE TRENT & MERSEY CANAL

JOHN MERRILL DAY CHALLENGE WALKS -
WHITE PEAK CHALLENGE WALK
DARK PEAK CHALLENGE WALK
PEAK DISTRICT END TO END WALKS
STAFFORDSHIRE MOORLANDS CHALLENGE WALK
THE LITTLE JOHN CHALLENGE WALK
YORKSHIRE DALES CHALLENGE WALK
NORTH YORKSHIRE MOORS CHALLENGE WALK
LAKELAND CHALLENGE WALK

INSTRUCTION & RECORD -
HIKE TO BE FIT.....STROLLING WITH JOHN
THE JOHN MERRILL WALK RECORD BOOK

MULTIPLE DAY WALKS -
THE RIVERS'S WAY
PEAK DISTRICT: HIGH LEVEL ROUTE
PEAK DISTRICT MARATHONS
THE LIMEY WAY
THE PEAKLAND WAY

COAST WALKS & NATIONAL TRAILS -
ISLE OF WIGHT COAST PATH
PEMBROKESHIRE COAST PATH
THE CLEVELAND WAY

PEAK DISTRICT HISTORICAL GUIDES -
DERBYSHIRE INNS - an A to Z guide
HALLS AND CASTLES OF THE PEAK DISTRICT & DERBYSHIRE
TOURING THE PEAK DISTRICT & DERBYSHIRE BY CAR
DERBYSHIRE FOLKLORE
PUNISHMENT IN DERBYSHIRE
CUSTOMS OF THE PEAK DISTRICT & DERBYSHIRE
WINSTER - a souvenir guide
ARKWRIGHT OF CROMFORD
TALES FROM THE MINES by Geoffrey Carr
PEAK DISTRICT PLACE NAMES by Martin Spray

JOHN MERRILL'S MAJOR WALKS -
TURN RIGHT AT LAND'S END
WITH MUSTARD ON MY BACK
TURN RIGHT AT DEATH VALLEY
EMERALD COAST WALK

COLOUR GUIDES -
THE PEAK DISTRICT.........Something to remember her by.

SKETCH BOOKS -
NORTH STAFFORDSHIRE SKETCHBOOK by John Creber

IN PREPARATION -
LONG CIRCULAR WALKS IN STAFFORDSHIRE
SHORT CIRCULAR WALKS IN WEST YORKSHIRE
SHORT CIRCULAR WALKS IN THE YORKSHIRE DALES
SHORT CIRCULAR WALKS IN THE LAKE DISTRICT
SHORT CIRCULAR WALKS IN NORTH YORKSHIRE MOORS
RUTLAND WATER CHALLENGE WALK
SNOWDONIA CHALLENGE WALK
FOOTPATHS OF THE WORLD - Vol 1 - NORTH AMERICA
HIKING IN NEW MEXICO

☞ Full list from JNM PUBLICATIONS, Winster, Matlock, Derbys.

THE JOHN MERRILL WALK BADGE

Complete six of the walks in this book and get the above special walk badge. Badges are a black cloth with walking man embroidered in four colours and measure - 3 1/2" in diameter.

BADGE ORDER FORM

Date and details of walks completed ....

....

NAME ....

ADDRESS ....

....
Price: £2.00 each including postage, VAT and signed completion certificate. Amount enclosed (Payable to JNM Publications) ....
From: JNM PUBLICATIONS, Winster, Matlock,
Derbyshire. DE4 2DQ.
✆ Winster (062988) 454 - 24hr answering service.
FAX: Winster (062988) 416

************ YOU MAY PHOTOCOPY THIS FORM ************

"I'VE DONE A JOHN MERRILL WALK" T SHIRT - Emerald Green with white lettering and walking man logo. Send £5.50 to JNM Publications stating size required.

WALK RECORD CHART

DATE WALKED

CASTLETON – 4 miles.. ⬭

HATHERSAGE – 3 miles... ⬭

EYAM – 2 miles... ⬭

TIDESWELL – 2 miles... ⬭

BUXTON – 2 1/2 miles.. ⬭

BAKEWELL – 2 miles... ⬭

YOULGREAVE – 1 1/2 miles....................................... ⬭

WINSTER – 2 miles... ⬭

CROMFORD – 3 miles... ⬭

WIRKSWORTH – 3 miles.. ⬭

TISSINGTON – 1 1/2 miles.. ⬭

ASHBOURNE – 2 miles.. ⬭

RIVER BRADFORD, YOULGREAVE.